WILSON®

READING SYSTEM

STUDENT READER SEVEN

THIRD EDITION

by Barbara A. Wilson

Wilson Language Training
175 West Main Street
Millbury, Massachusetts 01527-1441
(508) 865-5699

ISBN 1-56778-073-3 Student Reader Seven Item# SR7AB

THIRD EDITION

The Wilson Reading System is published by:

Wilson Language Training Corp.
175 West Main Street
Millbury, MA 01527-1441
United States of America Tel#(508) 865-5699

Printed in the U.S.A.

STEP

7

Concepts

Introduction to Sound Options, Contractions

7.1 - Sound options: c {e, i, y} (concentrate, concede)
g {e, i, y} (gentle, pungent)

7.2 - ge, ce, dge (lunge, indulgence, fudge)

7.3 - New trigraph and digraph: tch, ph (fetch, pamphlet)

7.4 - tion, sion (subtraction, expansion)

7.5 - contractions (we've, I'll)

pace	stage	rice
cent	place	price
cinch	twice	huge
face	spruce	spice
page	lace	gem

space	ice	age
lice	brace	nice
cage	embrace	decide
gentle	Bruce	giant
princess	slice	pencil

gentleman	recent	sincere
excite	recess	fancy
advice	city	Nancy
replace	Cindy	spicy
tragic	accept	citizen

stencil	priceless	suggest
excitement	magic	cancel
success	cycle	Grace
Celtics	spacecraft	concentrate
accident	gigantic	successful

crush	magic	grant
principal	segment	cancel
conduct	success	dragon
apology	confuse	cycle
engrave	price	mice

gusto	except	crisis
apologize	recognize	recite
captive	stage	rectangle
trace	trickle	stingy
concrete	twice	glare

truce	wage	rage
gene	cite	loge
ace	splice	grace
gibe	cell	tangent
process	vigil	decent

---

giblet	citrus	enrage
legend	civil	agent
gentry	gimlet	incite
civics	rampage	cogent
placid	abscess	pungent

---

precede	cypress	stingy
ingest	recede	angel
gyro	digest	dingy
oblige	gyrus	transcend
census	secede	gelatin

decency	regency	cyanide
agility	anticipate	citric
cyclone	concept	access
genetic	incident	vicinity
incentive	contingent	cyclops

congest	disgrace	innocent
fugitive	homicide	geologist
emancipate	longitude	potency
astringent	indulgent	deficit
gyrostat	infancy	centipede

reciprocate	contingency	engagement
vacancy	reconcile	indignant
tendency	magistrate	gin
diligent	legislate	engage
accent	concede	refuge

glade	decline	legend
designate	coma	gala
hiccup	civilize	agency
crescent	golden	rancid
agitate	cobra	ascend

---

acrid	thrice	gobble
racist	guzzle	capital
centrum	climax	coincide
adjacent	cult	gambrel
contribute	aggravate	agitate

---

gelt	blace	gint
cilt	cest	boce
prace	struge	gilb
glest	clem	ploge
geft	cide	gump

clim	ceff	grote
cimp	ging	crin
gede	gend	cipe
cere	cive	frage
gind	fice	bloge

plogy	comlige	cynet
flegent	occint	glomece
crintage	trinpoce	filcy
celtone	decepe	regist
centope	trimcel	tringy

plevice	dilgene	gintly
trincy	ginmope	brency
regage	gytrone	placent
stengil	receme	gymote
inscroge	centrome	gromece

1. We must replace the old vehicle.

2. This lunch is much too spicy.

3. My pencil is not in my desk.

4. Steve had to get a brace on his leg after he fell off the cycle.

5. Jane was frequently complimented on her nice, fancy dress.

6. Is there space in the old shed for this giant cage?

7. Hopefully, Jim will do magic for the kids.

8. The tragic accident happened because of carelessness.

9. Gram is finished with the dress – lace and all!

10. I request complete quiet so that I can concentrate to finish this task.

1. Bob suggested that Teddy can play baseball in the spring.
2. Tim jumped up and gave his mom a huge embrace.
3. Jill requested that her dad tell her the tale of the princess.
4. Cindy likes to assemble the puzzles.
5. The excitement left us all in a daze.
6. Be gentle with the little puppy.
7. This test is not a cinch, it is a struggle!
8. Did Jake fumble the ball in the game at recess?
9. Find your place in line, and then we will go to class.
10. That stage is for the magic show.

1. What will the wages be for that job?
2. Hopefully, we can replace the missing baseball.
3. The lime gelatin is in the mold.
4. My engagement ring is lost!
5. Nancy did not like to gamble a cent.
6. Jim is quite restless to find out the price of the condo in Boston.
7. I think that price will enrage him!
8. Regretfully, I must cancel my next date with Ed so that I can complete this job.
9. The boss wished that Tom was finished with the last page.
10. I think Jenna's rude comments were disgraceful.

St. our could first again

1. That tent is our place of refuge.

2. Cindy wished that she could be a secret agent.

3. The cops witnessed the incident on Gentome St.

4. Ed thinks that the Celtics will clinch first place again.

5. Dad wisely expressed his advice.

6. Mom was quite congested, so she had to go to the clinic.

7. The delinquents went on a rampage and demolished the stage set.

8. Dad insisted that he would make the giblet gravy.

9. We will get a small refund when we recycle these cans.

10. That concept is quite difficult to grasp.

our keep Mr. could break

1. Did the travel agency send us our plane tickets?
2. Our company must struggle to keep pace in this competitive city.
3. There is a distinctive spice in this cake, but I cannot identify it.
4. Bob has a decent job at the Centrum.
5. Mr. Hopkins could be a secret agent.
6. I hope we find a place of refuge so that I can rest!
7. Nancy and Bill are quite stingy and refuse to help the rest of the family.
8. Ted has been unable to acquire access to the files.
9. Recess is a requirement so you must give the students a break.
10. The democratic process is quite complex.

1. Jake sincerely hopes that Wendy will go on a date with him.
2. The engagement of Gene and Eva was quite unexpected!
3. Benny was found innocent of all crimes.
4. I will be indulgent after the basketball game and go get ice cream.
5. Melissa's date, Cedric, was quite a gentleman.
6. The kids could not decide, so Mr. Billings suggested a democratic vote.
7. James is a U.S. citizen, but his wife is a citizen of Finland.
8. Tammy witnessed the escape of a fugitive.
9. That student is in the adjacent class.
10. The geologist lost the rock sample in the vicinity of that second cave.

Magic

At recess time, a man came to the class to do magic. Mike said that he could figure it out. He felt it would be a cinch. Tony said, "O.K. then, let's wage a bet." Mike accepted.

The man on stage began his magic. He had a princess doll in a cage. He chanted a tune and held a cloth over the cage. When he lifted it, the cage was gone and he held a giant pencil. It was impossible to guess! The man did the trick twice. Mike did concentrate, but he could not figure it out. Tony was glad to win the bet.

Space Age Skit

Students at the Belmont School were planning skits for Class Day. Jenny was a ham, but Cathy did not wish to be in the skit. Jenny said to her friend, "No problem! It will be a cinch. You will love it on stage!"

The skit was called "Space Age." Twice, Cathy wanted to quit, but Jenny insisted that she do it. On the day of the skit, Cathy's hands felt like ice. She did not want to face the crowd.

The Space Age skit was the last to go on stage. Cathy did it! She was so glad to finish it with pride. It was a huge success.

been similar already Cincinatti would

Fugitive Rampage

The detectives were called to investigate. The agent came to the scene to find expensive gems stolen from a home in the city of Los Angeles. Despite extensive planning, a trespasser had been able to get entry.

Recently, there were many such crimes in fine L.A. homes. The detectives suspected a fugitive who had gone on a similar rampage in Cincinatti. One innocent citizen had been killed already. Hopefully they could prevent any more tragic incidents.

Nancy's Braces

Nancy's dentist suggested that she get braces. Nancy did not expect this advice. Her dentist sincerely felt braces would be an effective way to prevent problems. He would have to extract a tooth to make more space.

Nancy asked about the price of the braces. It was a disgrace! They were quite expensive. She felt like she was too old, as well. She was twenty-six and had recently begun a sales job. She did not want braces to upset her smile.

Nancy had to decide. Most of the cost would be refundable. She could not let her age prevent her if it would be best in the long-run. She restlessly mulled it over. Her husband successfully convinced her that it would not be bad. The dentist told her that she would not regret it. At last, Nancy set the date to have it done.

nce

advance	glance	dance
France	sentence	since
balance	ambulance	fence
Lance	prince	prance
license	Constance	chance

nge, nce

challenge	trance	absence
confidence	wince	hinge
evidence	excellence	plunge
advance	silence	entrance
fringe	convince	distance

smudge	dodge	badge
trudge	lodge	hedge
edge	fudge	bridge
budge	ridge	ledge
nudge	judge	hodgepodge

A

sledge	drudge	fledge
dredge	wedge	sludge
pudge	abridge	begrudge
grudge	Madge	kedge
dislodge	Midge	pledge

B

abundance	imbalance	dunce
abstinence	hence	essence
innocence	intelligence	adolescence
lance	ambivalence	credence
condolence	enhance	commence

whence	thence	sustenance
presence	residence	nonce
stance	Providence	negligence
substance	romance	province
hesitance	resistance	pittance

avenge	cringe	revenge
binge	lozenge	springe
lunge	scavenge	tinge
twinge	unhinge	bulge
divulge	indulge	bilge

trance	tinge	flange
instance	diligence	sixpence
infringe	fragrance	expunge
lance	cadence	singe
scrunge	existence	impinge

1. Sandra was able to run the distance in the race.
2. I like the tulips along that white fence.
3. Jim drove until he could find the entrance to the mall.
4. Dad has to help Hank construct a fence.
5. A square dance will be held at the lodge on July 10th.
6. Mr. Prince requested complete silence, but the class did not stop talking.
7. Since the race, Tom has not run any distance at all.
8. I like the fringe on the sides of that dress.
9. The requirements of the class present a huge challenge to the students.
10. Jane helped me convince Sandra to go on the fast amusement ride.

1. The bridge made from blocks did not crumble.
2. We elected a judge for the contest.
3. The rattle is on the edge of the table.
4. Trudge across the puddle to the dry side of the path.
5. Tony gave his pal a nudge.
6. Hopefully, I can get some fudge at the shop.
7. The ball is stuck in the vent and it will not budge.
8. You need a badge to get into the big event.
9. The kids like to play dodge ball at recess.
10. Carefully, James inched along the rocky ledge.

1. We will relocate this company to the city of Providence.
2. Kate has lots of confidence, but her date, Tom, is quite shy.
3. You should establish a sequence of skills.
4. The detective must find more evidence for his most recent case.
5. I think his residence is in our province.
6. At his wife's insistence, Ted went to the job agency for help.
7. Henry asked Betsy for advice on which kind of fragrance to buy for Emma.
8. Ron was thankful when his boss gave him a big cash advance.
9. The existence of the will helped solve all the family disputes.
10. This publishing project has instilled more confidence in Ed.

1. I want to indulge in a fattening, vanilla ice cream cone!
2. Suddenly, the cop had to lunge at the gunman in the bank hold-up.
3. I plan on witnessing the big event when Bob and Tim plunge into the icy, cold pond.
4. That lemon lozenge will help my sore throat.
5. The president will divulge his plan to balance the budget.
6. I still cringe when I hear that song.
7. Our basketball team hopes to get revenge.
8. The animals will scavenge in the trash unless we get the lid back on the can.
9. I think this dish will be best if we tinge it with more spice.
10. The bilge of the ship must be lifted out of the water.

her money for piece against too you

dge

1. Tammy sat at the edge of her bed to contemplate what to do next.
2. There will be a hodgepodge of items for sale to make money for softball.
3. Cindy did not want to smudge her make-up, so she would not jump in the lake.
4. Madge had a bridge game at the club.
5. If you win the bet it will entitle you to a huge piece of fudge.
6. The judge must sentence the juvenile delinquent.
7. It is regretful that Mr. Plonce holds such a grudge against his dad.
8. Mom will not budge from her position that the investment will be too costly.
9. Madge has incredible intelligence, but it is sometimes hidden by her shyness.
10. The cops must dredge the small pond.

The Princess Dance

Constance had dance lessons ever since she was five years old. Now she was ten. She wanted a challenge so she decided to convince her mom to let her enter the big dance contest. She had to dance for a judge.

The big event came at last. Constance dressed like a princess. There was silence when she came on the stage. Then the music began. Constance did her dance. She had lots of confidence. Afterwards she sat on the edge of her seat as the judge gave her score. She did not win but she still had lots of fun. She was glad that she did her princess dance.

The Elk's Lodge

The Elk's lodge had become a bit run-down. Randy suggested that each member contribute to fix the place. If they accepted the challenge, then Randy had confidence that the job could be completed by June. He did not anticipate any problems since the job was small.

Randy gave evidence that the lodge needed repair. The entrance hall was dingy, the fence along the drive was broken and the shingles needed paint. At his insistence, the Elks finally did decide to make the repairs. The lodge did not need to be fancy, but it would be nice to spruce it up.

loved stay because purchase each see could her new afford

Indulgence

Madge loved extravagance! Since she and Steve invested in the condo, she wished to get expensive items to fill it. Steve told her that they could not afford such indulgences, but he did not convince her.

Madge was able to get many things and still stay within the budget. She felt it was a thrilling challenge. Madge told Steve about each new item in advance. Most of the time Steve was fond of the prospective purchase as well.

In time, Steve could see that Madge was entirely respectful of the budget. This did silence his protests, and Madge had fun as she expressively filled her home.

itch	match	pitch
switch	catch	crutches
ditch	kitchen	pitcher
sketch	catcher	ketchup
switch	scratch	witch

ph

Joseph	dolphin	telephone
alphabet	Philip	phone
atmosphere	triumph	trophy
photo	Ralph	phonics
photograph	pamphlet	digraph

batch	notch	stitch
splotch	Dutch	flitch
etch	patch	latch
stretch	snitch	hatch
crutch	glitch	thatch

ratch	hutch	scotch
blotch	ketch	twitch
snatch	botch	fetch
ratchet	stitches	dispatch
Gretchen	satchel	Mitchell

sphere	graph	humph
phase	emphasis	cellophane
phonograph	prophet	phrase
phosphate	stratosphere	aphid
monograph	geography	phantom

sphinx	emphatic	graphite
hyphen	phosphide	graphic
emphasize	photon	phony
photocell	photocopy	philosophy
prophesy	phonology	phlox

could

tch

1. Tim had a big scratch on his leg from the tomcat.
2. Sam drenched his hot dog in ketchup!
3. Since Randy could not catch the ball, the dog had to fetch it.
4. Who will pitch in the next baseball game?
5. You can hitch the wagon to the back of that truck.
6. Ed checked the time on the kitchen clock.
7. Did the witch costume scare the kids?
8. Did Sandy chuckle when Jim spilled the ketchup on his pants?
9. I munched on the last batch of chicken wings.
10. Ben struck his nose on a rock when he fell in the ditch.

see again for letters our you

ph

1. The kids wanted to go see the dolphins again.
2. Joseph can juggle five balls but Rudolph can juggle six.
3. Who will win the trophy for the best project?
4. Philip wishfully asked for a drum set.
5. Can you name the letters in the alphabet.
6. The phone is ringing in the kitchen.
7. Will you share that handful of photographs?
8. Our baseball win was such a triumph.
9. We must not pollute the atmosphere.
10. Gretchen had no difficulty finishing the big stack of pancakes.

1. The catcher did not juggle the ball when the pitcher tossed a wild pitch.
2. The Dutch clock was demolished when it struck the table.
3. The kids sat in amazement as Tom did his sketch.
4. Ralph did not like the telephone call he had at lunchtime.
5. Kim had to stretch after she ran around the track ten times.
6. We must hang this shamrock in the kitchen to celebrate St. Patrick's Day.
7. Mitchell had lipstick on his neck!
8. It will take us a long time to bake this batch of clams.
9. The cops had the kid empty his pockets on the hatchback trunk.
10. I had to get stitches when I had the baseball accident.

1. Ted made the best tackle in the Thanksgiving Day match.
2. Fred held the trump ace in the game of pitch, so he felt quite confident.
3. Next, the boss will dispatch the vans to pick up the junk.
4. Did the Dutch and English settle in that colony?
5. Sandra was still on crutches from her accident last June.
6. Helpfully, Gram will stitch up this dress for the banquet.
7. Did Ted find the hatchet in the old shed?
8. I will not go to the dance because I am so itchy from the sun.
9. Bev gave Pam a kitchen witch that matched her red drapes.
10. Ralph just wanted to stretch out on the cot, but he had to make lunch.

1. Joseph suggested that we go see his prospective land investment.
2. I hope I do not flunk the geography quiz.
3. Lately, Bob has been rude; I hope it is just a phase!
4. When the Celtics triumph, the fans in Boston go wild!
5. Philip had to ask his dad for advice about his old Dodge van.
6. The phone call established a contact with the big company.
7. James was quite upset when he lost the photograph of Wendy.
8. I must get cellophane next time I shop.
9. Mom was grateful when Dad helped Randolph with the alphabet.
10. We will send you a pamphlet to describe the retirement plan.

outside chair turn hospital light sprain floor someone over could else

tch

Gretchen's Visit

Gretchen and Philip Smith went to visit the Mitchells. They sat outside and grilled hotdogs. Gretchen wished to be helpful and went into the kitchen for the bottle of ketchup. She could not find the switch to turn on the light.

All of a sudden, there was a big crash. Philip and the Mitchells ran to the kitchen. Gretchen was on the floor with the hutch on top of her leg! Phil and Tom Mitchell had to hustle over and lift it off her.

Gretchen could only hobble to a chair. Her ankle was red and swelling. She did not want to go to the hospital, but she did.

At nine o'clock, Gretchen limped back into the Mitchell's kitchen. This time she was on crutches! She was quite thankful that her ankle was not broken. The accident had resulted in a bad sprain.

"I'm all set for a hot dog," Gretchen said. "But this time, I'll let someone else get the bottle of ketchup!"

Dolphin Land

Ralph gave Joseph a telephone call. He had a pamphlet from Dolphin Land. The travel agency sent a photograph as well.

Ralph and Joseph felt it would be fun to go. They spent the day at Dolphin Land. They were able to get many photographs. The dolphins did a dance and many other tricks. The day at dolphin land was lots of fun.

Joseph Tackles the Stack

Joseph had to attack the complex graph for his job. He had a stack of documents that he had to tackle and compile before Monday. He intended to finally complete this phase of the project.

Joseph got a tall glass of lemonade and hid from the T.V. He went out on the deck where he could not be distracted by the ballgame. He put on an old phonograph. He had to stick to the job until it was complete.

Joseph did not go back inside until five o'clock. He was glad to have a decent graph to submit to his boss. He missed the game, but he finished the difficult task on time.

subtraction	instruction	solution
fiction	prevention	location
protection	education	promotion
infection	mention	dictation
temptation	emotion	relaxation

illustration	description	invention
lotion	question	pollution
position	production	condition
addition	competition	definition
suggestion	nation	recommendation

sion

mansion	expansion	comprehension
discussion	expression	concussion
invasion	collision	occasion
confusion	conclusion	explosion
decision	division	television

A

---

tion

constitution	prescription	reception
introduction	conjunction	satisfaction
locomotion	execution	congestion
devotion	digestion	adoption
eruption	objection	option

B

---

pacification	unification	ratification
notification	gratification	colonization
capitalization	intensification	regimentation
manifestation	exemplification	hospitalization
rehabilitation	monopolization	representation

---

ventilation	regulation	indication
registration	calculation	cultivation
combination	isolation	education
notification	indication	solidification
electrification	humanization	excommunication

---

a-tion

inflation	indignation	commendation
constellation	implication	ramification
stabilization	civilization	specification
notification	utilization	modification
minimization	codification	edification

---

i-tion

imposition	nutrition	ignition
volition	munition	suction
locomotion	cognition	contrition
petition	opposition	disposition
expedition	condition	definition

---

intention	reproduction	investigation
consumption	sensation	salvation
mutation	probation	digestion
exemption	traction	vocation
domination	consolation	suction

application	reclamation	desolation
elocution	delegation	exultation
quotation	condensation	abduction
conjunction	conviction	fixation
addiction	excretion	infraction

n-sion
l-sion

pension	tension	impulsion
compulsion	suspension	extension
convulsion	dissension	ascension
pretension	repulsion	revulsion
expulsion	propulsion	dimension

---

declension	reprehension	recension
apprehension	condescension	expansionist
pensioned	declension	distension
dimension	dimensionless	incomprehension
emulsion	pretension	misapprehension

---

passion	mission	session
fission	cession	confession
admission	regression	depression
progression	repression	digression
commission	concession	aggression

impression	impassion	submission
remission	recession	omission
profession	succession	compassion
obsession	possession	oppression
concussion	discussion	procession

/zhun/

vision	fusion	lesion
abrasion	intrusion	exclusion
illusion	precision	evasion
provision	protrusion	cohesion
revision	adhesion	obtrusion

diffusion	allusion	incision
implosion	collusion	transfusion
invasion	precision	misprision
exclusion	inclusion	protrusion
explosion	infusion	erosion

you for out about

tion

1. Randy did not mention my phone call.
2. Mr. Wall gave instructions for the quiz.
3. I will think of a solution to your problem.
4. Let's find out the exact location of the dolphins.
5. We will convince Dad to get a dog for protection.
6. Put that lotion on when you go in the sun.
7. Joseph will ask the question about the spelling test.
8. Do you know the definition of smudge?
9. With just a little instruction, I was able to win at tennis.
10. When I complete the addition, will you do the subtraction?

1. Tommy's red van was in a collision.
2. The students jumped at the explosion.
3. The invasion of the tribe was tragic.
4. Mom plans to have a discussion with me.
5. The expression on Kendra's face made me smile.
6. The mansion on the hill is quite impressive.
7. Toby got a bad concussion when he fell off his bike.
8. There was a lot of confusion after the explosion.
9. Phil willingly helped lift the television onto the van.
10. It will be a big occasion when the princess visits this nation.

1. I think the pollution in this city is disgusting!
2. I felt a strong emotion in my chest.
3. The Smiths will be able to host a reception for Mr. Cosby.
4. I think the rental option is the best plan.
5. The salesman handed out pamphlets as an introduction to his product.
6. Relocation is the only solution to our company's space problem.
7. Bill made the suggestion that we travel to the lake for some relaxation.
8. The detective must conduct an intensive investigation into that difficult case.
9. The plan must present some options so that the boss can make a selection.
10. Danny was given a big promotion after his successful trip to China.

for

tion

1. Ben had to complete the job application and then hope for the best.
2. Jim and Peg felt the temptation to travel to Africa.
3. There is condensation on this glass.
4. Tom helped with the music production for that rock band.
5. It was difficult to get a description of the useful invention.
6. Steve's drug addiction is so sad.
7. That company will have a liquidation sale and I expect we will be able to find a desk.
8. Is my visit an imposition?
9. The witness will hopefully give a consistent description of the delinquent.
10. The Wisconsin clinic intends to present topics on nutrition in the month of June.

after Mrs. reading for books about because team

sion

1. Madge willingly went to the bridge game held at the gentleman's mansion.
2. Joseph will get a decent pension after his retirement.
3. Jane innocently asked a question that left tension in the club.
4. The kids in Mrs. Billing's class will use the reading comprehension books.
5. Bob had to take exact dimensions to make a kitchen cabinet for his wife.
6. The company is planning a big expansion in late spring.
7. Joseph had to ask his boss for an extension on the publishing project.
8. Jane and Bob have a little apprehension about the sale.
9. Jake was given a suspension for his disrespectful attitude.
10. The loss was because of the bad dissension on the team.

about for blood their another Olympics

/zhun/

1. Mitchell completely lost his vision in the bad accident.
2. The men had to carefully plan the invasion into the jungle.
3. Edna had to provide the Navy with their provisions.
4. Mr. Jones will have a blood transfusion to prevent another attack.
5. The conclusion of the Olympics will be an impressive event.
6. The boss will make his decision about the contract this month.
7. Jake will get a big fine for tax evasion.
8. Kendall was upset about the intrusion.
9. I have an abrasion on my leg from the incident.
10. The precision of that vehicle is impressive.

1. Dad has compassion for those made helpless by the tragic quake in Mexico.
2. Jane wished that she had help with the math calculations.
3. The club engaged in exclusion by establishing a policy which discriminated by race.
4. Tony had to sit in isolation because he disrupted the class.
5. Babs got such satisfaction when her students made excellent progress.
6. Joseph had to find the definition of the word "illusion."
7. The regulations for education in this state are quite complex.
8. Nancy must check the collision policy she has on the van.
9. Jake wanted to give Madge the notification of her new position.
10. I think Ted will get a suspension for cutting class again.

1. Betsy had a bad abrasion on her leg.
2. The delinquent gave his confession to the detective.
3. Regretfully, the discussion did not seem to help Pam's confidence.
4. The king is adept with his delegation of duty.
5. I asked the boss for a concrete definition of my role here.
6. Cathy's new car handles with precision.
7. Jane gave no indication of her plans when she quit her job.
8. Cindy must decide if she will accept that position at the bank.
9. When the tickets went on sale at the Centrum, there was a lot of confusion.
10. Jim had no intention of missing class, but his van got a flat tire.

out day knew work meet saw read stood somehow office herself

A Position in Judge Phillip's Office

Cindy Mitchell filled out an application for a job in the office of Judge Sandra Phillips. The judge was kind, and Cindy felt that it would be exciting to work in her office. Cindy had confidence that she could do the job. She had the intention to somehow secure the position.

Cindy had to figure out a plan. She knew that a reception was to be held at the city hall. Judge Phillips would be attending it. Cindy made plans to go and introduce herself to the judge. She would mention her hope for the office job. Possibly she could convince the judge to hire her for the open position. She felt the excitement of anticipation.

Cindy went to the reception with her plan in mind. She did not wish to be an imposition on Judge Phillips, yet she intended to meet her. At last Cindy saw the judge standing alone. She went up to her and held out her hand. The judge recognized her face but could not place her. Quickly, Cindy told her that she was an applicant for the office position. Sandra Phillips was impressed with Ms. Mitchell's confidence and determination.

The next day, Judge Phillips went to her office. She had many applications. One name stood out – Cindy Mitchell. The judge carefully read the application. She was happy.

The judge picked up the phone to make the call to Ms. Mitchell. Cindy gladly accepted the job.

jeep busy soon about out again

Tom and Meg's Bronco

Jim and Tom went for a ride in Tom's Bronco jeep. Since the last trip, it had not run well. Jim suggested that the transmission had a problem. This made Tom upset.

When Tom and Jim got back home, Tom told his wife, Meg. She did not want to replace the transmission. They could not spend much cash to fix the Bronco. They had to hope that it was not a big problem.

Tom went to the gas station with the Bronco to find out about its condition. The place was quite busy, and the man could not check it out until after lunch.

At last, a diagnosis was made. It was not the transmission! It would be a cinch to fix. Tom and Meg were quite glad. The price of the job was not very much. Soon the Bronco was in fine shape again.

The Price of Progress

Teddy's boss, Mr. Lance, called him into his office. He wanted to send Teddy on a mission to find out about their competition. A copy and print shop was opening across the street!

Teddy went to the new shop. It was not open yet, but the door was unlocked. Teddy made the decision to go in. He gave the impression that he wanted a printing job done.

The shop was quite impressive! It had twice the equipment as Mr. Lance's little shop. Teddy left it feeling quite sad. He did not want to tell his boss.

When Teddy went back to his shop, he could see the apprehension on Mr. Lance's face. Teddy's expression said it all. He did not even tell his boss about the new place. Mr. Lance just went into his office and quietly shut the door.

Decision to Shop

Jane got a call from her friend, Betty. Betty wanted to go shopping at the mall. Usually, Jane would go, but she was just getting set to see the conclusion of a movie called The Last Invasion from Space. Jane made the decision to see the final segment since she had spent the evening before watching the beginning.

Jane asked Betty if she wanted to visit and see the movie. Betty did not like television but she occasionally watched it. She did not wish to see The Last Invasion from Space but she felt it would be nice to see Jane.

Betty drove across the city to Jane's apartment. Jane had her jacket on and met Betty at the door. "There is a revision in the plan," said Jane. "We can shop after all. There is some confusion with programming, so the movie's conclusion will be on tomorrow night.

isn't	hasn't	haven't
didn't	hadn't	can't
doesn't	wasn't	weren't
wouldn't	shouldn't	couldn't
aren't	don't	won't

he's	she's	it's
that's	who's	what's
there's	here's	let's
you'll	they'll	we'll
he'll	I'll	she'll

you've	they've	we've
I've	I'd	she'd
he'd	we'd	they'd
you're	we're	they're
I'm	I've	I'd

---

there's	haven't	she'll
weren't	that's	don't
I've	who's	I'd
couldn't	you're	we'll
won't	we're	aren't

---

1. Ben can't go to the fiddle contest until he finishes the dishes.
2. Joseph won't be able to fly on that plane.
3. I'll be gone on vacation for some time.
4. I didn't see the best invention at the state-wide contest.
5. Cindy said that you're able to visit Mr. Sanchez in the hospital.
6. I think we'll get plenty of sunshine.
7. What's in the pot on the stove?
8. Willis shouldn't travel since he is sick.
9. Let's try to juggle these five balls like the lady did at the festival.
10. She'll get the bottle for Linda.

for

1. I couldn't do the last subtraction problem.
2. We haven't finished the picnic lunch that Jason packed for us.
3. Who's the strongest kid in this class?
4. Malcolm doesn't have the price for that item.
5. I'd like to have some fudge but it is so expensive.
6. What's that on the bridge?
7. Ralph didn't go fishing and Jane didn't swim.
8. Let's stack up this pile of bricks behind the shed.
9. I don't like pickles so I won't take any on my plate.
10. We've had lots of bad luck lately.

1. There hasn't been much production at the company lately.
2. They'll make the decision about the quiz.
3. That investigation can't take place until the evidence is collected for this case.
4. We'll have to get advice before we travel.
5. Who's equipment is in the middle of the path?
6. Brad couldn't make his sales quota.
7. Let's request time off when we finish this project.
8. Frank hasn't mentioned the photograph.
9. Gretchen doesn't like to spend time in the kitchen.
10. Sandra has sensitive skin and shouldn't be in the sun.

Mary and Dennis

Mary hasn't seen her husband, Dennis, in two weeks. She misses him terribly! He's at his job and won't be back for yet another week. Mary wasn't able to get time off to go with him. She's in school and couldn't go. This doesn't happen often, and Mary's* glad of that! She'll be much more content when Dennis gets home. She's happy with his constant company and is lonely now without him.

*Mary's = Mary is

Post Test Step Seven

A

question	gentle	they'll
silence	can't	concentrate
replace	scratch	don't
photograph	instruction	dodge
who's	you're	plunge

B

pungent	diligence	hyphen
we've	dispatch	progression
centipede	specification	adjacent
infection	cellophane	trudge
gyrostat	infringe	intrusion

Post Test Step Seven

!@#$%

ronvince	strudge	rovision
fincantation	phosphile	litch
nivision	demission	bation
tringy	ginmope	boce
cimp	comlige	stimgage

1. Put an s above c's that say /s/.
2. Put a j above g's that say /j/.
3. Put an f above any digraph that says /f/ and underline the digraph.
4. Underline trigraphs and mark the preceding vowel with a breve (˘).
5. Put a circle around /shun/ sounds and a box around /zhun/ sounds.
6. Identify the two words made into any contraction.